The
Story
Tree
Tales to Read Aloud

In memory of my grandparents and their brothers and sisters:
Luptons, Ransomes, Gees and Lloyds (storytellers all) — H. L.

For Rebecca and Giacomo, Zoë and Gala — S. F.

Barefoot Books
PO Box 95
Kingswood
Bristol
BS30 5BH

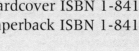

This book was typeset in Kidprint, Dolores and Meridien

The illustrations were prepared in mixed medium

Graphic design by Polka. Creation, Bath
Colour separation by Grafiscan, Verona
Printed and bound in Singapore by Tien Wah Press

This book is printed on 100% acid-free paper

Hardcover ISBN 1-84148-311-7
Paperback ISBN 1-84148-313-3

British Cataloguing-in-Publication Data: a catalogue record for this
book is available from the British Library

1 3 5 7 9 8 6 4 2

The Story Tree

Tales to Read Aloud

Retold by Hugh Lupton
Illustrated by Sophie Fatus

Barefoot Books
better books for children

CONTENTS

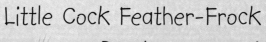

The Three Billy Goats Gruff
Norwegian

The Little Red Hen
English

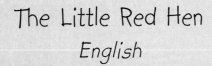

The Blue Coat
Jewish

Sources
and Acknowledgements

The Magic Porridge Pot
German

ONCE UPON A TIME there lived a little girl and her mother. Once upon a time there lived a little girl and her mother and they were hungry. The cupboards were empty, the shelves were empty and their bellies were empty.

So the little girl took an empty basket and she walked out of the house and out of the village to see what she could find. She walked for a long time, and she walked for a very long time, until she saw a tangle of bramble bushes covered with fat blackberries.

'These are what we need!'

She picked and she picked until the bushes were bare and her basket was full. Then she turned on her heel and she set off for home. She walked for a long time, and she walked for a very long time, but just as she was drawing close to home she met an old woman.

Thin as a scarecrow that old woman was, dressed in rags and tatters, her face as wrinkled as an old winter's apple. She looked at the little girl and she smiled a toothless smile.

'Those are lovely fat bramble blackberries you have in your basket, my child. You couldn't spare a handful, could you, for an old grandmother without a tooth in her gums nor a penny to her name?'

7

The little girl looked at the poor old
woman and she forgot how hungry she was.
   'Of course I can,' she said. 'You can eat
as many as you like!'
   She held up the basket, and the old woman
dipped her shaking hand into the blackberries and scooped them into her mouth.

'Mmmm, those are good blackberries,
and you are a good girl with a kind and a
tender heart. And because you've been good
to me, I'll be good to you.'

8

The old woman reached beneath the rags and tatters of her shawl and pulled out a black iron pot. She pressed it into the girl's hands. 'Here's a present for you, my child. It is a magic pot. Put it on the table when you get home and say, "Boil, Pot, Boil", and it'll give you all the porridge you can eat. When you've had your fill, just say, "Stop, Pot, Stop". Do you understand?'

The little girl looked into the pot. 'Yes,' she said, 'and thank you.' But when she looked up the old woman was gone. So she went home with the iron pot and the basket of blackberries.

Her mother was very pleased to see her, and even more pleased when the little girl put the iron pot on to the table and said, 'Boil, Pot, Boil.'

Straight away it was bubbling over with porridge. They filled one bowl, they filled another, and then the little girl said, 'Stop, Pot, Stop.'

And the iron pot was as clean and black and empty as before. They fetched spoons and tasted the porridge. It was delicious, creamy and sweet, and when they stirred the blackberries into it – well, it was the best meal they had tasted in their lives. They went to bed that night with their bellies full and smiles on their faces. And from that day onwards, whenever they were hungry, the little girl would say, 'Boil, Pot, Boil', and there would be porridge in plenty, and 'Stop, Pot, Stop', when they'd had their fill.

All was well and good until one day when the little girl's mother said, 'Do you remember that time when we had blackberries with our porridge? Do you remember how good it tasted?'

And the little girl said, 'Yes, I remember, and if you like I'll go and pick some more.'

11

She took the empty basket and she walked out of the house and out of the village. She walked for a long time, and she walked for a very long time, until she came to the tangle of brambles with their new crop of fat blackberries, and she began to pick.

But while she was away her mother was sitting at home, looking at the black iron pot on the table, and the more she looked at it the hungrier she felt. 'I'll just have one little bowlful,' she thought. 'Just to pass the time.'

12

She fetched her bowl and turned
to the pot. 'Boil, Pot, Boil.'
Straight away the pot was
bubbling over with steaming porridge.
She filled her bowl to the brim.
'Stop!'

But the pot didn't stop. More and more
porridge was bubbling over the rim – soon
the table was covered in porridge. She
picked up a spoon and hit the pot.
'STOP!'
But the pot didn't stop. Soon the
porridge was dripping on to the floor.
'PLEASE STOP!'
But the pot didn't stop. The floor was
covered, the steaming porridge was flowing
out of the door. She climbed on to a chair.
'PLEASE, PLEASE, STOP!'

13

But the pot didn't stop. Soon the whole village was covered with porridge.
People were climbing on to tables; they were climbing up stairs.
'PLEASE, PLEASE, PLEASE STOP!'
But the pot didn't stop.
When the little girl came home at the end of the day, with her basket full
of fat blackberries, she saw a flood of steaming porridge lapping the
gutters of the roofs of the houses, and all the people clinging to the chimneys.
'TELL THAT POT TO STOP!' they shouted.

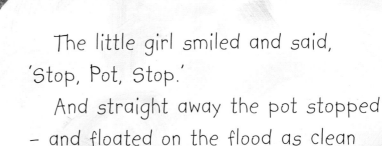

The little girl smiled and said,
'Stop, Pot, Stop.'

And straight away the pot stopped
– and floated on the flood as clean
and black and empty as before.

The little girl sat down at the edge
of the flood of porridge. She poured
her blackberries on to it, she stirred
them with her finger, and she scooped
up handfuls of the delicious mixture
and gulped it down.

As for her mother and the other
people of the village – well, they had to
eat their way indoors, but they didn't
mind. After all, it was the sweetest,
creamiest porridge in the world.

And that was the end of that story.

15

Monkey-See, Monkey-Do
Indian

ONCE UPON A TIME there was a man who sold hats.
Once upon a time there was a man who sold hats, and he
was pushing his cart along a road through the jungle.

And what was in his cart? Hats, of course! There were
top hats, mob caps, bobble hats, flat caps, billy-cocks and
bonnets, balaclavas and bowler hats, all carefully packed
together and ready for market.
But there was a hole in the road.
One of the wheels of the cart got
caught and the cart tipped over.
It tipped right over and all the
hats spilled this way and that
way on to the road.

Now, in the trees of that jungle there lived hundreds of monkeys, and when they saw all those hats lying in the road they came laughing and chattering and swinging down from the branches. Each one of them grabbed a hat and put it on his head.

Before the man could shout 'Stop!' all his hats had been taken. The only one left was the hat he was wearing on his own head.

17

He looked up into the trees. On every branch there was a monkey with a hat. There were monkeys with top hats, monkeys with mob caps, monkeys with *bobble* hats, monkeys with flat caps, monkeys with billy-cocks and bonnets, balaclavas and bowlers. They were all looking down at him.

The man was cross! He put his hands to his mouth and shouted up at them, 'Give me back my hats!'

But what a monkey sees, a monkey does. They all put their hands to their mouths and shouted back at him.

The man *was* angry! He picked up a stick and waved it at them. 'Give me back my hats or there'll be trouble!'

But what a monkey sees, a monkey does. They all broke sticks from the branches and waved them back at him.

19

The man was *furious*!
He stamped on the ground
with his feet. 'Give me back
my hats or there'll be
double-trouble!'

But what a monkey sees, a
monkey does. They all stamped
their feet and bellowed back at him.
The man was sad. He buried his
face in his hands and began to cry.
'Oh, my precious hats. How will I
ever get you back?'

But what a monkey sees, a monkey
does. They all buried their faces in their
hands and sobbed back at him.

20

The man looked up at the monkeys. The monkeys looked down at the man.

Suddenly, the man pulled the hat from his head and hurled it down on to the ground. 'Well, that's enough of that! No more selling hats for me! I'll have to find myself another job!'

He lifted the wheel out of its hole and pushed his empty cart away along the road.

But what a monkey sees, a monkey does. They all pulled their hats from their heads, hurled them down on to the ground and scampered away into the shadows of the jungle.

And when the man looked over his shoulder, what did he see? Hats, of course, lying in the road: top hats, mob caps, bobble hats, flat caps, billy-cocks and bonnets, balaclavas and bowler hats. He ran back and loaded them carefully into his cart. Then he put his own hat on to his own head and pushed his cart along the road towards the market.

And that was the end of that story.

The Sweetest Song

African-American

ONCE UPON A TIME Little Daughter
was picking flowers. Once upon a time Little Daughter
was picking flowers on the far side of the fence. Her
papa had told her not to. Her mama had told her not
to. But her papa and her mama weren't watching
and Little Daughter had seen a beautiful
yellow flower nodding in the breeze just
beyond the fence.

'No harm in opening the gate and picking
one little yellow flower,' she thought to herself.

24

Then she saw a red one, farther away, shining like a little flame.

'No harm in picking a red one to put with the yellow one.'

Then she saw some blue flowers, farther away again.

'No harm in putting the blues with the red and yellow.'

Soon the fence and gate were far behind her and she had a bunch of flowers in her hand. It was shining and shining with such yellows and reds and blues and purples and pinks that she started to sing with happiness.

'Tray-bla, tray-bla, cum qua, Kimo.'

25

Suddenly she felt a
shadow. She looked up and
saw a wolf – a great grey
wolf looking down at her
with its yellow eyes.

The wolf opened its
mouth and spoke.

'Sing that sweetest,
goodest song again.'

So Little Daughter sang
the song again.

'Tray-bla, tray-bla,
cum qua, Kimo.'

And as she sang, the great grey wolf closed his
eyes and smiled. And as she sang, Little Daughter
tiptoed, tiptoed back towards the gate.

26

As soon as the song
was over, the wolf opened
his eyes and came bounding,
bounding behind her.

'Did you move?'

'Oh no,' said Little Daughter. 'Oh no,
dear wolf, why should I move?'

'Why indeed?' said the wolf. 'Now sing
me that sweetest, goodest song again.'

So Little Daughter sang the song again.

'Tray-bla, tray-bla, cum qua, kimo.'
And as she sang, the great grey wolf closed his eyes and smiled.
And Little Daughter tiptoed, tiptoed back towards the gate.

As soon as the song was over
the wolf opened his eyes and
came bounding, bounding behind her.
  'Did you move?'
  'Oh no, dear wolf, why should I move?'
  'Why indeed? Now sing me that
sweetest, goodest song one
more time again.'
  So Little Daughter sang
the song again.

29

'Tray-bla, tray-bla, cum qua, Kimo.'
And the great grey wolf closed his
eyes and smiled.

Little Daughter tiptoed, tiptoed
back to the gate, and through the gate.

And as soon as the song was over, the wolf opened
his eyes and came bounding, bounding behind her.
But 'click' the gate was shut, and 'clack' the
gate was locked, and Little Daughter was safe.
Little Daughter was sweetest, goodest safe
inside, with a bunch of bright flowers in her fist.
    And that was the end of that story.

Little Cock Feather-Frock
Russian

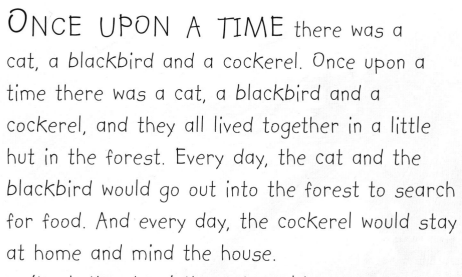

ONCE UPON A TIME there was a cat, a blackbird and a cockerel. Once upon a time there was a cat, a blackbird and a cockerel, and they all lived together in a little hut in the forest. Every day, the cat and the blackbird would go out into the forest to search for food. And every day, the cockerel would stay at home and mind the house.

'Lock the door,' the cat would say.

'Sit by the stove,' the blackbird would say.

'And if Old Foxy comes knocking at the door, *don't* let him in,' they both said together.

Well, the days passed and the weeks passed and all was well and good until one fine morning when Old Foxy *did* come knocking at the door.

Knock, knock, knock, Little Cock Feather-Frock,
A pea would be yours if you unlocked the doors.

The cockerel loved peas, and the chance of a sweet, green pea straight from the pod was too good to miss. He stepped across the floor and, clack-click, he opened the door – and Old Foxy scooped him into his sack.

'Into my sack, on to my back, my sweet little feathery supper!'

33

The poor cockerel began to shout, 'Help, help, brother blackbird, dear Cat Cotonaevitch, Old Foxy has scooped me into his sack. He's carrying me off to the back of beyond for his sweet little feathery supper!'

Then the cat and the blackbird, who were not far from the little hut, heard the cockerel and they chased Old Foxy away. And soon the cockerel was safe home, crooning and preening his ruffled feathers.

The next morning, the cat said, 'Lock the doors.'

And the blackbird said, 'Sit by the stove.'

And they both said, 'And if Old Foxy comes knocking at the door, *don't* let him in.'

But they hadn't been gone for long when Old Foxy *did* come knocking at the door.

Knock, knock, knock, Little Cock Feather-Frock,
A nut would be yours if you opened the doors.

The cockerel loved nuts, and the chance of a sweet, brown hazelnut straight from the shell was too good to miss. He stepped across the floor and, clack-click, he opened the door – and Old Foxy scooped him into his sack.

'Into my sack, on to my back, my sweet little feathery supper!'

'Help, help, brother blackbird, dear Cat Cotonaevitch, Old Foxy has scooped me into his sack. He's carrying me off to the back of beyond for his sweet little feathery supper!'

This time the cat and the blackbird had gone a long way from home in search of food, but they heard the cockerel's voice, very faintly, and they chased Old Foxy away. And soon the cockerel was safe home, crooning and preening his ruffled feathers.

35

The next morning it was the same again.
'Lock the doors.'
'Sit by the stove.'
'And if Old Foxy comes knocking at the door,
don't let him in.'
But, sure enough, Old Foxy *did* come knocking
at the door.

Knock, knock, knock, Little Cock Feather-Frock,
A loaf would be yours if you opened the doors.

The cockerel loved bread, and the chance of a sweet,
fresh loaf straight from the oven was too good to miss.
He stepped across the floor and, clack-click, he opened
the door – and old Foxy scooped him into his sack.
'Into my sack, on to my back, my sweet little feathery supper!'

'Help, help, brother blackbird, dear Cat Cotonaevitch, Old Foxy has scooped me into his sack. He's carrying me off to the back of beyond for his sweet little feathery supper!'

But this time the cat and the blackbird had gone a long, long way from home in search of food. They were so far away that they didn't hear the cockerel shouting. And when they came back to the hut at the end of the day, the door was open and the cockerel was gone.

Oh dear, oh dear.

They looked here and there, and soon enough they saw Old Foxy's footprints on the ground.

They followed those footprints, through forests and over mountains, until they came to the back of beyond, and the footprints led straight to the door of Old Foxy's house. The cat and the blackbird began to sing,

Foxy, dear Foxy, are you within?
Your two old sisters are come visiting.

Well, inside the house, Old Foxy had put the cockerel on to a plate and he was just sharpening his teeth and making ready to eat his supper when he heard the song. He pricked up his ears and he listened again.

Foxy, dear Foxy, are you within?
Your two old sisters are come visiting.

'That's strange,' Old Foxy thought to himself. 'I didn't think I had any sisters.'

He stepped across the floor and, clack-click, he opened the door – and the cat scratched his nose, the blackbird scratched his eyes and the cockerel jumped from the plate and pecked his red tail from behind. And Old Foxy was so afraid that he turned and ran away. He ran and he ran from the back of beyond, and he was never seen again. And as for the cat, the blackbird and the cockerel – they journeyed back over mountains and through forests, until they were safe home in the little hut. And soon enough Little Cock Feather-Frock was crooning and preening his ruffled feathers. And as far as I know he still is. And that was the end of that story.

39

The Three Billy Goats Gruff
Norwegian

ONCE UPON A TIME
there were three Billy Goats Gruff.
Once upon a time there were three Billy
Goats Gruff and they were making a
journey to the green hill where the
grass grows thickest and sweetest.
On their way they came to a high
bridge over a deep river. Under that
bridge there lived a knobbledy
troll, as old and as cold
as a boulder of stone.

First of all came the youngest Billy Goat Gruff, lifting up his hooves and trip-trap, trip-trap, trip-trapping over the bridge. The troll's ears twitched, his nose wrinkled and his mouth opened. 'WHO'S THAT trip-trapping over my bridge?'

'It's only me, the littlest Billy Goat Gruff. I'm going to the green hill to eat and eat and make myself fat.'

The troll licked his grey lips with his red tongue. 'I'm coming to gobble you up!'

'Oh no, Mr Troll, I'm much too small. Why don't you wait for the second Billy Goat Gruff? He's far bigger than me.'

'Very well,' grunted the troll. 'Away with you!'

41

So off he trotted, and soon he was nibbling the thick, sweet grass on the green hill.

A little while later came the second Billy Goat Gruff, lifting up his hooves and TRIP-TRAP, TRIP-TRAP, TRIP-TRAPPING over the bridge. The troll's ears twitched, his nose wrinkled and his mouth opened. 'WHO'S THAT trip-trapping over my bridge?'

'It's only me, the middle-sized Billy Goat Gruff. I'm going
to the green hill to eat and eat and make myself fat.'
The troll licked his grey lips with his red tongue.
'I'm coming to gobble you up!'

43

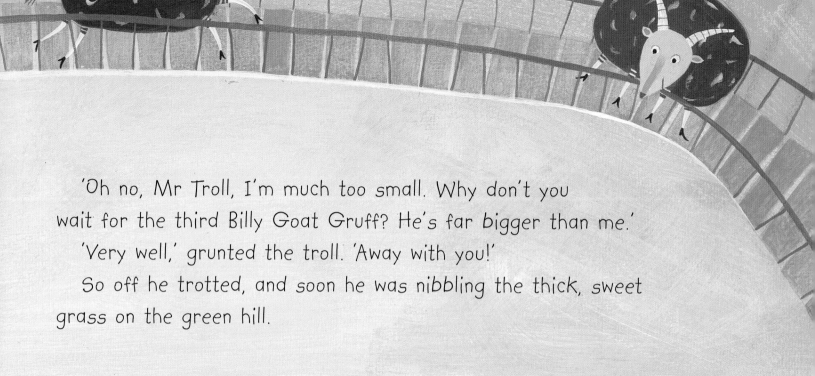

'Oh no, Mr Troll, I'm much too small. Why don't you wait for the third Billy Goat Gruff? He's far bigger than me.'

'Very well,' grunted the troll. 'Away with you!'

So off he trotted, and soon he was nibbling the thick, sweet grass on the green hill.

A little while later came the third Billy Goat
Gruff, lifting up his hooves and TRIP-TRAP,
TRIP-TRAP, TRIP-TRAPPING over the bridge.
The troll's ears twitched, his nose wrinkled and his
mouth opened. 'WHO'S THAT trip-trapping
over my bridge?'

'It's only me, the biggest Billy Goat Gruff. I'm
going to the green hill to eat and eat and make
myself fat.'

The troll licked his grey lips with his red tongue.
'I'm coming to gobble you up!'

But the biggest Billy Goat Gruff lowered
his head and said,

'Come along, Mr Troll, and gobble your fill.
I've got two horns, as sharp as thorns,
That'll toss you over the hill!'

46

And when the troll came clambering up over the side of the bridge, the Billy Goat charged and caught him on the sharp prongs of his horns, and tossed his head so that the troll was thrown high up into the sky, and then hard down on to the ground far beyond the green hill. And that was the end of him.

And as for the three Billy Goats Gruff – if they aren't fat yet, then they're munching still at the thick, sweet grass on the green hill.

And that was the end of that story.

The Little Red Hen
English

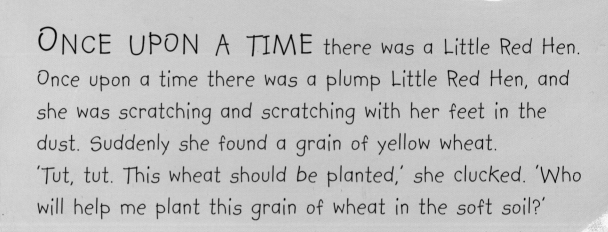

ONCE UPON A TIME there was a Little Red Hen.
Once upon a time there was a plump Little Red Hen, and
she was scratching and scratching with her feet in the
dust. Suddenly she found a grain of yellow wheat.
'Tut, tut. This wheat should be planted,' she clucked. 'Who
will help me plant this grain of wheat in the soft soil?'

'Not I,' said Dab the duck.

'Not I,' said Tib the cat.
'Not I,' said Tod the fox.

'Well then, I'll plant it myself,'
said the Little Red Hen. And she did.

Soon enough the grain had grown into a tall stalk with a long ear of yellow wheat at the top of it.

'Tut, tut. This wheat is ripe,' she clucked. 'Who will help me cut it?'

'Not I,' said Dab the duck.

'Not I,' said Tib the cat.

'Not I,' said Tod the fox.

'Well then, I'll cut it myself,' said the Little Red Hen. And she did.

Soon enough the ear of yellow wheat was lying at her feet.

'Tut, tut. This ear is ready
for threshing,' she clucked.
'Who will help me thresh it?'
  'Not I,' said Dab the duck.
  'Not I,' said Tib the cat.
  'Not I,' said Tod the fox.

'Well then, I'll thresh it myself,'
said the Little Red Hen. And she did.

51

Soon enough the wheat was threshed and she'd blown away all the chaff with the flapping of her wings. 'Tut, tut. This wheat is ready for milling,' she clucked. 'Who will help me mill it into flour?'

'Not I,' said Dab the duck.
'Not I,' said Tib the cat.
'Not I,' said Tod the fox.

52

'Well then, I'll mill it myself,' said the Little Red Hen. And she did.

Soon enough the wheat had been milled between two stones into fine, soft flour.

'Tut, tut. This flour is ready for baking,' she clucked. 'Who will help me bake it into bread?'

'Not I,' said Dab the duck.
'Not I,' said Tib the cat.
'Not I,' said Tod the fox.

53

'Well then, I'll bake it myself,' said the Little Red Hen. And she did.

Soon enough it was mixed and kneaded and baked into a loaf of sweet, fresh, steaming bread.

'Tut, tut. This bread is ready for eating,' she clucked. 'Who will help me to eat it?'

'I will,' said Tib the cat.

'I will,' said Dab the duck.

'I will,' said Tod the fox.

'Oh no, you won't,' said the Little Red
Hen. 'I planted it all by myself. I cut it
all by myself. I threshed it and milled it
and baked it all by myself...and now I'm
going to eat it all by myself.'

And she did.

And that was the end of that story.

The Blue Coat
Jewish

ONCE UPON A TIME there was a boy called Tom.
Once upon a time there was a boy called Tom, and he didn't
have a coat to wear.

'Oh dear, oh dear,' his mother said, 'I'll have to make
you one.' So she went to the shop and bought a length of
blue cloth. She laid it out on a table and she set to work.

All day she worked and worked, cutting and shaping and fitting one part to another part, and she made him a beautiful coat. Tom was so pleased with it that he wore that blue coat in sunshine and snow, in rain and wind. He ran and jumped and splashed and rolled in it.

But then one day his mother looked him up and down.

'Oh dear, oh dear,' she said, 'that coat is tattered and torn beyond all redemption!'

57

She laid the blue coat out on a table and she set to work. All day she worked and worked, cutting out the best bits and shaping them together, fitting one part to another part, and she made him a beautiful waistcoat.

Tom was so pleased with it that he wore that blue waistcoat in sunshine and snow, in rain and wind. He ran and jumped and splashed and rolled in it.

But then one day his mother
looked him up and down.
   'Oh dear, oh dear,' she said,
'that waistcoat is tattered and torn
beyond all redemption!'
   She laid the blue waistcoat out
on a table and she set to work.

59

All day she worked and worked, cutting out the best bits and shaping them together, fitting one part to another part, and she made him a beautiful hat.

Tom was so pleased with it that he wore that blue hat in sunshine and snow, in rain and wind. He ran and jumped and splashed and rolled in it.

But one day his mother looked him up and down.

'Oh dear, oh dear,' she said, 'that hat is tattered and torn beyond all redemption!' She laid the blue hat out on a table and she set to work.

All day she worked and worked, cutting out the best bits and shaping them together, fitting one part to another part, and she made him a beautiful bow-tie.

Tom was so pleased with it that he wore that blue bow-tie in sunshine and snow, in rain and wind. He ran and jumped and splashed and rolled in it.

But then one day his mother looked him up and down.

'Oh dear, oh dear,' she said, 'that bow-tie is tattered and torn beyond all redemption!'

61

She laid the blue bow-tie out on a table and she set to work. All day she worked and worked, cutting out the best bits and shaping them together, fitting one part to another part, and she made him a beautiful button.

Tom was so pleased with it that he wore that blue button in sunshine and snow, in rain and wind. He ran and jumped and splashed and rolled with it.

62

But then one day his mother
looked him up and down.
'Oh dear, oh dear,' she said,
'that button is tattered and
torn beyond all redemption!'

She put the blue button on to a table and
she set to work. All day she worked and
worked, cutting out the best bits and shaping
them together, fitting one part to another
part, and she made him a beautiful story.
She made him the story of the Blue Coat
– and I've just told it to you!

SOURCES
and
ACKNOWLEDGEMENTS

Some of these tales have strayed further from the original sources than others in the process of retelling. That's the way of the oral tradition. Behind the storyteller is the chain of voices that have carried the tales through time. Sometimes that oral process polishes a tale to a perfection that doesn't need much in the way of addition or alteration.

THE MAGIC PORRIDGE POT

This old favourite comes from *Grimm's Fairy Tales* where it appears as 'Sweet Porridge' (*The Complete Grimm's Fairy Tales*, R & K Paul, London, 1975).

MONKEY-SEE, MONKEY-DO

I've always known this story and I'm sure there are plenty of printed versions, but I'm not familiar with them.

THE SWEETEST SONG

I found this story in Virginia Hamilton's magnificent collection of American Black Folktales, *The People Could Fly* (Random House, New York, 1985). A delightful book, both for its text and for Leo and Diane Dillon's illustrations.

LITTLE COCK FEATHER-FROCK

This story appears in Aleksandr Afanasiev's *Russian Fairy Tales* as 'The Cat, the Cock and the Fox' (Pantheon Fairy Tale Library, Pantheon Books, New York, 1975) where it doesn't have such a happy ending! This version also owes a debt to Helen East's reworking of it in her lovely collection *The Singing Sack* (A & C Black, London, 1989), a collection of song-stories with accompanying musical notation.

THE THREE BILLY GOATS GRUFF

Another old favourite, originally from George Dasent's translations of Asbjornsen and Moe's collection of Norwegian Fairy Tales (*Norse Fairy Tales*, G W Dasent, S T Freemantle, London, 1910). There is not, to my knowledge, a complete collection of Asbjornsen and Moe's *Norwegian Fairy Tales* available in English, but the Pantheon Folklore Library has published a selection (Pantheon, New York, 1960).

THE LITTLE RED HEN

I found this English tale in Raymond Briggs' *The Fairy Tale Treasury* (Hamish Hamilton, London, 1972). It cites Joseph Jacobs' *English Fairy Tales* (Bodley Head, London, 1968) as its source. I couldn't find it in my copy, but don't let that put you off getting hold of it, it's the definitive collection of English tales!

THE BLUE COAT

This story has become very popular among British storytellers. I can't remember whether I first heard it from my friend and fellow storyteller Taffy Thomas or from the great Scottish teller Duncan Williamson. The only written version I've seen was in the wonderful American magazine of myth and meaning, *Parabola*.

Barefoot Books
better books for children

At Barefoot Books, we celebrate art and story with books that open
the hearts and minds of children from all walks of life, inspiring them to read
deeper, search further, and explore their own creative gifts. Taking our
inspiration from many different cultures, we focus on themes that encourage
independence of spirit, enthusiasm for learning, and acceptance of other
traditions. Thoughtfully prepared by writers, artists and storytellers from
all over the world, our products combine the best of the present with the best
of the past to educate our children as the caretakers of tomorrow.

www.barefootbooks.com